Woodbourne Library
Washington-Centerville Public Library
Centerville, Ohio
DISCARD
W9-ACP-491

Bronislaw Huberman:

From Child Prodigy to Hero, the Violinist who saved Jewish Musicians from the Holocaust

Peter Aronson

Copyright © 2018 Peter Aronson

Double M Books Inc., New York

Woodbourne Library
Washington-Centerville Public Library
Centerville, Ohio

Double M Books Inc.
New York
The Groundbreaker Series is a registered trademark of Double M Books Inc.

peteraronsonbooks.com
peteraronsonbooks@gmail.com

Copyright © 2018 by Peter Aronson
All rights reserved

Library of Congress Cataloging-in-Publication Data

ISBN 978-1-7320775-0-8 (ebook)
ISBN 978-1-7320775-1-5 (print)

Front and back cover designs by Ashley Byland of Redbird Designs

Layout and formatting by Polgarus Studio

Printed in the United States of America

This book is dedicated to the many individuals who saved lives during the Holocaust.

Contents

Prologue

There are many heroic stories about World War II and the Holocaust. Countless articles, books and movies have told the tales of resistance fighters, average citizens, businessmen, diplomats, neighbors and nuns who risked their lives to protect and save Jews from the Nazis in Germany and other parts of Europe.

The story in this book also is about a hero, but a hero of a different kind. Bronislaw Huberman didn't risk his life. But he had the intelligence and foresight to realize in the 1930s that Jews had to leave Germany and other countries in Europe to live a prosperous, safe and fulfilling life. He didn't know at the time – no one really knew – that the Holocaust was coming. This is the story of Bronislaw Huberman and the founding of a Jewish orchestra in Palestine.

Bronislaw Huberman:

From Child Prodigy to Hero, the Violinist who saved Jewish Musicians from the Holocaust

Young Bronislaw Huberman (Wikimedia Commons)

On a beautiful spring day in 1891, in a small town in Poland, the sound of chirping birds mixed with the beautiful music of Beethoven. On this day, Bronislaw Huberman was doing what he loved to do every day of his young life – he was at home playing his violin.

Young Huberman loved to play the violin so much and he played it so beautifully, that one day he would make history – history that would be heard around the globe.

Bronislaw Huberman would perform before kings and queens and before adoring fans all over the world. But he also would become an outspoken advocate for human rights and peace. As an adult, with the world heading towards World War II, his violin became his sword. He became a musical miracle worker in a crumbling world. He would become one of the greatest violinists in the world and also a hero — for saving Jewish musicians from the Holocaust.

The Story of Young Huberman

(Courtesy of Rob Huberman)

The story of Bronislaw Huberman begins with his music and fame as a child. He was born in the small Polish town of Czestochowa on December 19, 1882. His father was a lawyer's assistant and an amateur musician. He desperately wanted his son to be a professional musician. By age 9, Huberman was helping support his parents and two brothers by performing in health spas in Austria and Germany.

At a special recital in Vienna, Huberman performed so beautifully that he was commanded to perform for Emperor Franz Joseph of Austria, the ruler of the country. The Emperor was so impressed with the young violinist that he presented him with a valuable violin.

As a child, Huberman became an international star. (Courtesy of Rob Huberman)

As word spread about the prodigy, he began performing throughout Western Europe – in France, Belgium, Germany, Austria and England – and even in the United States.

Huberman performing for Brahms and other famous composers at a concert in 1896. (Silhouette drawing by Otto Bohler, from An Orchestra is Born - A Monument to Bronislaw Huberman)

In 1896, at age 13, Huberman played 10 sold-out concerts in Vienna. One concert became legend. He performed Brahms' Violin Concerto with four of the world's greatest composers in the audience: Gustav Mahler, Anton Bruckner, Johann Strauss and Johannes Brahms himself. Brahms and the others wanted to witness this child prodigy for themselves. Huberman played so beautifully that Brahms, reportedly, cried with joy. After the concert, Brahms hugged and kissed young Huberman and gave him an autographed picture.

Brahms gave Huberman this autographed photograph, after seeing him perform.
(From An Orchestra is Born -A Monument to Bronislaw Huberman)

Huberman Matures into One of the Greatest Violinists in the World – and also becomes an outspoken Humanitarian

(Courtesy of Rob Huberman)

Over the years, Huberman would mature from child prodigy to one of the great violinists of the 20th Century. He became an internationally famous musician, playing all over the world. He cared about those who suffered. When a terrible earthquake struck Messina, Italy, in 1908, Huberman gave a concert to raise money to help the victims.

(Wikimedia Commons)

Then came the horrors of World War I. This would change Huberman's life forever. Huberman was in Berlin performing when the war broke out. Because he was Polish, he was considered an enemy of the state of Germany. He was arrested. The German crown princess, who loved Huberman's music, immediately got Huberman released from prison. But this episode led Huberman to realize that art – *his art, his music* - can overcome war and hatred. He became an outspoken pacifist.

Huberman began writing and speaking out as part of an anti-war group called the Pan Europeanists. They believed Europe should be like the United States, one big country with no foreign boundaries, instead of many separate countries. "Where there are no boundaries there are also no wars," Huberman wrote.

Huberman's political interests grew. He was Jewish. He began performing in Palestine, a faraway land on the beautiful Mediterranean Sea where Jews by the thousands were moving to escape anti-Semitism in Europe. Huberman played in theaters in Tel Aviv and Jerusalem and also on stages set up on the fields of agricultural settlements called kibbutzim. He witnessed the building of a country and a people's love of culture.

Huberman in Palestine on Kibbutz Ein Harod, in a later photo.
(Photo by Ida lbbeken, Courtesy of the Murray S. Katz Photo
Archives of the Israel Philharmonic Orchestra)

"One has the feeling as if with every new orange tree planted in the ground a parallel tree of spiritual culture was planted too," Huberman said in a speech in Jerusalem. He loved playing his music in Palestine.

Hitler and the Nazis
Take Over Germany

Hitler at a rally in 1933. (Wikimedia Commons)

As Huberman's love of Palestine grew, Hitler rose to power in Germany. The year was 1933. The Nazi government began discriminating against Jews. Jewish shops and businesses were boycotted. Many Jews were fired from their jobs, including Jewish musicians. They were forbidden from performing in the great orchestras of Germany.

Jews forced to march with anti-Semitic signs in Germany in 1933.
(Wikimedia Commons)

"One day a musician was a respected member of society and the next day he was in the gutter helpless," recalled David Grunschlag, a Jewish musician who would later go to Palestine.

Nazis ordered a boycott of Jewish shops in Germany in 1933. (Wikimedia Commons)

Another Jewish musician, Uri Toeplitz, recalled the Nazi soldiers blocking customers from entering Jewish shops and the painted Stars of David on the shop windows. Restaurants in Frankfurt, Germany, he said, had signs posted - "No Jews."

Huberman was deeply troubled by these events. He had loved Germany and had performed as a soloist for many years with the best German orchestras. Wilhelm Furtwängler, the famous German conductor, personally invited Huberman to return to Germany to perform with the Berlin Philharmonic Orchestra.

Wilhelm Furtwängler conducting in Berlin. (Wikimedia Commons)

This presented a great dilemma for Huberman. Most Jewish musicians in Germany were barred from playing with the best orchestras. Yet Huberman, a Jew, was being invited to play in Germany because he was one of the greatest violinists in the world.

Huberman responded to Furtwängler by writing an angry letter that was published in *The New York Times* on September 14, 1933. He rejected Furtwängler's offer to perform in Germany with the Berlin Philharmonic Orchestra. He criticized Germany's racist policy of eliminating German Jews from German music. He said he would not return to Germany to perform until Germany stopped discriminating against Jews.

Huberman Takes Action to Save Jewish Musicians; Einstein Comes to the Rescue

B ut life got worse, not better, for the Jews in Germany and other countries in mainland Europe. Huberman decided he had to take action to help the Jewish musicians. He wrote letters. He met with Jewish officials in Palestine. He knew the Jews in Palestine loved classical music. He knew they appreciated culture. He told officials he would start a new orchestra in Palestine, to allow the Jewish musicians to escape from Hitler and the Nazis.

"To beat the world campaign of anti-Semitism, it's not enough to create material and idealistic prosperity in Palestine," he wrote in a letter in support of his plan. "[T]he symphony orchestra as I visualize it would be perhaps the first and easiest step to the highest aim of Jewish humanity."

To Colonel Kisch, Haifa

These are the figures from my American drive:
  Donations $ 15,500, allotments $ 2000, pledges $ 7,000 etc.(U.S. dollars).
  Financial matters: Expenses £ 17,730, Income £ 21,860 (Engl. £).
  I think we are now in a position and therefore in an obligation to pay the following 12 months' salaries:

 4 leaders 1st violin and cello per month £20=£ 80
 6 leaders 2nd violin, viola, contrabass £16=£ 96
10 wind instruments and 1 harp, each at £15=£165
17 wind instruments at an average of £13=£221
31 string instruments other than leaders £13=£403
the salaries for non-permanent substitutes
for special occasions, such as Toscanini etc.   £ 50
 1 Orchestra attendant   £ 10
Office and Management staff   £ 60
Expenses for sheet music, brass instruments and perhaps contra-basses, which usually the orchestra organisation has to provide for the players, are not charged here. But on the other hand some income mentioned before is not discounted.

Huberman's letter detailing fundraising and expenses for the orchestra.
(From An Orchestra is Born - A Monument to Bronislaw Huberman)

Huberman began planning. He needed to raise $80,000 (about $1.5 million in today's dollars) to pay for instruments, salaries and musicians' travel from Europe to Palestine. This is when Huberman's violin became his sword. Huberman began performing feverishly across Europe and America to raise money.

In the United States, he gave 42 concerts in 60 days. But he could not raise enough money. So he turned for help to the most famous Jew in the world, Albert Einstein, the great German-Jewish scientist. Einstein had recently fled Germany to live in the United States.

Huberman and Albert Einstein, in a later photo. Huberman asked Einstein to help him raise money for the orchestra. (Photo by John Huberman, courtesy of Joan Payne)

Huberman wrote to Einstein: Because of "the German Barbarity… Palestine is provided with an otherwise unimaginable opportunity to get a cultural institution that's destined to serve as a model to the rest of the world." Huberman met with Einstein. Soon after, Einstein, along with others, helped Huberman raise enough money for the orchestra. But Huberman's work was far from over.

The Nazis Spread Anti-Semitism Across Europe

Hitler in 1935, the year the Nuremberg Laws were passed in Germany. The laws established formal racist policies against the Jews. (Wikimedia Commons)

By 1936, the plight of the Jews in Germany and other parts of Eastern Europe was getting worse. More Jews were losing their jobs and suffering financially. The racist Nuremberg Laws had been passed, prohibiting marriage between Germans and Jews. Under the laws, Jews no longer were considered citizens of Germany. Jewish musicians were forced to play in orchestras only with Jews, called the Kulturbund. Many thousands of Jews wanted to leave Germany, including hundreds of Jewish musicians. Many musicians wanted to join Huberman's orchestra in Palestine, but there were positions for only about 50 from Europe. The vandalism and violence was spreading.

One musician recalled an attack on Jewish students at his school in Budapest, Hungary.

Lorand Fenyves, in 2000, recalled the Nazi attack on his school in Hungary.
(Photo by Peter Aronson)

"Fifteen to 20 young people came in with sacks filled with rocks and they beat up the Jews," recalled Lorand Fenyves, a 15-year-old music student at the time. His friend was thrown down the stairs and had to be hospitalized. "It was a terrible, terrible thing."

Fenyves said he survived because a man hid him in the ladies room and locked the door. The attack "was such a shock that I decided that very day that I had to leave the country," he said.

Musician Toeplitz recalled that his father, a prominent professor of mathematics at the University of Bonn, was fired by the Nazis, making life even more difficult.

As the anti-Semitism and violence spread across Europe, Huberman decided to select Jewish musicians from all over Europe. This made the auditions even more competitive, emotional and tense. Auditions were conducted in Germany, Hungary, Austria, Czechoslovakia and Poland - in hotels, in living rooms, wherever they could meet with musicians. Musicians were playing for their future and for their lives. Huberman had to make difficult choices, as many of the best musicians in Europe auditioned. He was under a lot of pressure. He insisted he would select only the best musicians, not friends or friends of friends.

Huberman was determined to make the Palestine Orchestra one of the world's best. "In art there can be no mercy and no compromise," he wrote to a friend. Huberman followed through on his promise. He made his selections. Musicians were notified.

"No question about it that he saved our lives," said musician Fenyves, a violinist. He said all the other Jewish students at his school died in the Holocaust, except for the three who went to Palestine.

Violence and Politics Endanger Huberman's Plan

Jewish residents being evacuated from the Old City in Jerusalem, in Palestine, during violence between Arabs and Jews in 1936. (Wikimedia Commons)

Huberman had made his selections for the orchestra. The musicians chosen included Lorand Fenyves, David Grunschlag and Uri Toeplitz. But as final plans were being made, Huberman's dream was thrown into doubt. Not by Hitler, but by violence between Arabs and Jews in Palestine. More than 300 people were killed in Palestine in 1936 alone. This tension between Arabs and Jews caused the British government, which ruled Palestine at the time, to cut the number of visas for Jews immigrating to Palestine. This meant the musicians might not be able to go live in Palestine. If they could not go to Palestine, there would be no orchestra. And the musicians would be forced to try to survive under Hitler and the Nazis.

"My nerves are close to a breakdown!" Huberman wrote to a friend, as pressure mounted against the orchestra.

Chaim Weizmann, left, and David Ben-Gurion helped Huberman establish his orchestra. (National Photo Collection of Israel, via Wikimedia Commons)

Huberman was desperate, so he sought help again from very powerful and important Jews. He wrote to the two most powerful Jews in Palestine, David Ben-Gurion, the Jewish leader, and Chaim Weizmann, president of the World Zionist Organization.

"… I will have spent two years moving heaven and earth in order to bring music to Palestine with an absolutely first-class symphony orchestra," Huberman wrote to Weizmann. "It would be a monstrous disgrace for all of us if the orchestra failed." The Jewish leaders studied the issue. In his leadership role, Weizmann fought for immigration for all Jews to Palestine. In the end, he made sure Huberman's musicians got their visas.

Huberman's Dream Comes True – and Toscanini Conducts!

Jewish musicians and their families, on board a ship travelling from Europe to Palestine in 1936. (Courtesy of Murray S. Katz Photo Archives of the Israel Philharmonic Orchestra)

In the fall of 1936, 53 Jewish musicians sailed by boat from Trieste, Italy, across the Mediterranean Sea to Palestine. It was a victorious journey for musicians escaping Hitler and the Nazis. They would now live in a free land, away from anti-Semitism and oppression. The musicians settled into their new life in Palestine. They were a close group, together often.

Jewish musicians, new members of the Palestine Orchestra, in 1936 after arriving in Palestine from Europe. (Courtesy of Murray S. Katz Photo Archives of the Israel Philharmonic Orchestra)

Huberman greeting conductor Arturo Toscanini in Palestine. (Wikimedia Commons)

Starting the orchestra was a major international event. It became even bigger news when it was announced that the most famous conductor in the world, Arturo Toscanini, would come to Palestine to conduct the orchestra's first concerts. The musicians were in awe of him.

Huberman, right, congratulates Toscanini after a rehearsal.
(Courtesy of Murray S. Katz Photo Archives of the Israel Philharmonic Orchestra)

"I don't need to tell you that Toscanini was a magician," recalled violinist Fenyves. "He hypnotized the orchestra. He didn't conduct the orchestra, he hypnotized the orchestra."

For Huberman, the orchestra's creation and Toscanini's involvement was cause for celebration.

(The Palestine Post)

The Palestine Orchestra's first concert was held on December 26, 1936, in Tel Aviv, before a crowd of 3,000 people dressed in evening gowns and tuxedos. So many people attended the concert that a large crowd of people who could not get tickets listened to the concert quietly from outside the theater.

By establishing the Palestine Orchestra, Bronislaw Huberman saved the lives of Jewish musicians and their families. Six million Jews would die in the Holocaust during World War II. An unknown number of those killed were Jewish orchestra musicians from Germany, Poland, Austria, Czechoslovakia, Hungary and elsewhere in Europe.

Soon after the State of Israel was established in Palestine in 1948, the Palestine Orchestra changed its name to the Israel Philharmonic Orchestra. Many great conductors have led the orchestra over the years, from Leonard Bernstein conducting hundreds of concerts to Zubin Mehta, the longtime music director for life. Today, the Israel Philharmonic Orchestra is one of the greatest orchestras in the world, and, as Huberman had hoped, the leading cultural ambassador for the state of Israel. Since 1936, the orchestra has played in more than 50 countries on five continents.

A young Leonard Bernstein leading the Israel Philharmonic Orchestra in 1948. (Courtesy of Murray S. Katz Photo Archives of the Israel Philharmonic Orchestra)

Zubin Mehta conducting the Israel Philharmonic Orchestra. (Photo by Oded Antman, Courtesy of the Murray S. Katz Photo Archives of the Israel Philharmonic Orchestra)

"Huberman had a dream that the orchestra should be so good to show the ... Nazis that we can do it better," recalled musician Toeplitz, who was a member of the orchestra for more than 30 years. He said Huberman more than fulfilled his dream by creating a great Jewish orchestra at the same time when Hitler's Germany was planning on destroying the Jews of Europe.

Street signs near the orchestra's theater are named in honor of Huberman and Toscanini. (Wikimedia Commons)

In Tel Aviv, a street near the orchestra's theater is named after Bronislaw Huberman. An adjacent street is named after Arturo Toscanini. Huberman is remembered as the founder of the Israel Philharmonic Orchestra and the savior of many Jewish musicians from the horror of the Holocaust.

Author's Postscript

Bronislaw Huberman's guests at the first concert were Chaim Weizmann and David Ben-Gurion, the founding fathers of the state of Israel. The orchestra was an immediate success. After the first series of concerts conducted by Toscanini, which included performances in Egypt, Toscanini said he was thrilled by the concerts and announced that he would conduct the orchestra during the next season as well.

Toscanini and Huberman in Haifa, Palestine, 1936. (Unknown photographer, courtesy of Murray S. Katz Photo Archives of the Israel Philharmonic Orchestra)

In its first season, the orchestra sold 6,300 ticket subscriptions in Tel Aviv, Jerusalem and Haifa, a huge number when considering that the Jewish population in those cities at the time was only 260,000. In addition, Huberman had insisted that the orchestra have a second series of concerts for the laborers, with ticket prices one fifth of the cost. These concerts sold out and the workers contributed 1,000 pounds from their unemployment insurance fund to help pay for the cost of renovating the orchestra's Tel Aviv theatre. Huberman could not contain his enthusiasm when writing to Einstein in 1937: "These figures give purely externally a picture of the relatively unexampled participation of the country in the new institution, but the frenzy of enthusiasm that gripped the entire land when the first concerts under Toscanini became reality cannot be described by any number, or by any words. It was just an atmosphere that lay beyond all other impressions aroused by art, even the highest art."

Poster advertising Palestine Orchestra concerts for 1937. (Courtesy of Rob Huberman)

Huberman travelled extensively for his concerts. (Courtesy of Rob Huberman)

Once the orchestra was underway, Huberman resumed his international performance schedule. However, Huberman remained intimately involved in even the smallest details of the orchestra, constantly writing instructions to orchestra management: advising on which music to perform and encouraging the use of proper acoustics in the theatres and proper housing for the musicians. And, of course, he was always involved in the never-ending task of fundraising for the orchestra, whether through his countless concerts or promotional interviews with newspapers.

A Jewish family in Warsaw, Poland, in 1943, being marched to deportation to a concentration camp. (Wikimedia Commons)

By September 1940, as World War II was breaking out in Europe, Huberman decided to settle in New York. He knew it was too dangerous for him to live in mainland Europe. In July 1941, Nazi leader Hermann Goering wrote to a leader of the SS: make "all necessary preparations with regard to organizational, substantive and financial viewpoints for a total solution of the Jewish question in German-occupied Europe." By September 1941, all Jews in Germany were required to wear the Star of David. By October 1941, all Jewish emigration from Germany stopped. Formal deportation of Jews to the concentration camps began in 1942. Nazi Germany's policy of exterminating the Jews in Europe was underway.

Huberman said in a fundraising speech in 1942, "What for Palestine meant a cultural institution of the highest importance, became an emergency rescue for the Jewish orchestra members of Central Europe."

During this time, Huberman became a full-fledged supporter of the Zionist movement, speaking out in favor of a Jewish state in Palestine.

After the war, Huberman had intended to return to Palestine, but he never did. He returned to Europe and on June 16, 1947, he died at his home in Nant sur Corsier, Switzerland. He was 64 years old.

Less than a year later, on May 14, 1948, the State of Israel declared its independence and the orchestra played Hatikva, the new country's national anthem, at the proclamation ceremony in Tel Aviv. The Israel Philharmonic Orchestra is considered one of the finest orchestras in the world. Since 1977, the orchestra has been lead by the internationally renowned conductor Zubin Mehta, the orchestra's music director for life. Bronislaw Huberman's dream not only came true, but it has flourished in the more than 80 years since the orchestra was founded.

The Israel Philharmonic Orchestra has been led by conductor Zubin Mehta for more than 40 years. (Photo by Shai Skiff, Courtesy of the Murray S. Katz Photo Archives of the Israel Philharmonic Orchestra)

Author's Note

I wish to thank Uzi Shalev for his friendship and help over the years on my Huberman project. It is through Uzi, an old friend from Kibbutz Ein Dor and a long-time bassoonist with the Israel Philharmonic Orchestra, that I discovered the Huberman story.

I also would like to thank the following individuals and organizations: Joan Payne, Bronislaw Huberman's granddaughter, for her kindness and access to letters and photographs; The Israel Philharmonic Orchestra and Avivit Hochstadter, the IPO's archives manager, for access to and permission to use photographs and archival material; Princeton University, for access to Albert Einstein's archive; and Rob Huberman, for permission to use items on his Huberman website.

I wish to thank original members of the Israel Philharmonic Orchestra for their time and willingness to talk with me. They include Lorand Fenyves, Uri Toeplitz, Abrasha Bor, Schlomo Bor, Felix Galimar, and Lotte Hammerschlag Bamberger. I also wish to thank

Maurice Surovitch, Paula Catell and Rosi and Toni Grunschlag for their kindness and allowing me to interview them.

Thanks to Ashley Byland of Redbird Designs, for her attractive front and back cover designs. She was very patient during the process.

Jason Anderson, of Polgarus Studio, deserves a lot of credit for his excellent format and design of the book. He also was very patient with me as we worked through the process.

I also wish to thank Jane Friedman for her helpful advice.

Finally, I wish to offer thanks and love to my family: my wife, Emily, and my daughters, Mabel and Maisy, for giving me their love and the time and encouragement needed to complete my writing projects.

Selected Bibliography

An Orchestra Is Born, A Monument to Bronislaw Huberman. Tel Aviv: Yachelav United Publishers Company Limited, 1969.

Fischer, Klaus P. *Nazi Germany: A New History.* New York: The Continuum Publishing Company, 1995.

Kater, Michael H. *The Twisted Muse: Musicians and Their Music in the Third Reich.* New York: Oxford University Press, 1997.

The New York Times, selected articles, 1896 through 1947.

Reifenberg-Rosenbaum, Adele. *Strad Magazine*, August 1947.

Schwartz, Boris. *Great Masters of the Violin.* New York: Simon and Schuster, 1983.

Shirer, William L. *The Rise and Fall of the Third Reich.* New York: Fawcett Crest, 1950.

Steinweis, Alan E. *Art, Ideology and Economics in Nazi Germany.* Chapel Hill, N.C.: The University of North Carolina Press, 1993.

Oral History Collection of the Israel Philharmonic Orchestra, selected interviews.

Websites

www.yadvasham.org, the website for Yad Vashem, The World Holocaust Remembrance Center, in Israel

www.ushmm.org, the website for the United States Holocaust Memorial Museum in Washington, D.C.

http://geocities.com/vienna/stasse/1162/huberman.html

http://ak.planet.gen.nz/~holsem/huberman/huberman.html

https://commons.wikimedia.org/wiki/Main_Page, for photographs in the public domain

BronislawHuberman.com

Also, additional material consulted included:

- The private letters of Bronislaw Huberman provided by his granddaughter, Joan Payne;

- Correspondence from and between Bronislaw Huberman and others who helped him start the orchestra, provided by the Israel Philharmonic Orchestra archive in Tel Aviv; and

- Private letters of Albert Einstein, provided by Princeton University.

Much of the research for this book was done while I was writing *A Musical Life*, a feature-length screenplay based on the story told in this book.

Photo Credits

1. Bronislaw Huberman as a young child. (Wikimedia Commons)

2. Huberman as an older child. (Courtesy of Rob Huberman)

3. Ad for young Huberman's first concert at Carnegie Hall in New York. (Courtesy of Rob Huberman)

4. Huberman performing for Brahms and other famous composers at a concert in 1896. (Silhouette drawing by Otto Bohler, from An Orchestra is Born - A Monument to Bronislaw Huberman)

5. A photograph of Brahms with his autograph, presented to Young Huberman. (From An Orchestra is Born - A Monument to Bronislaw Huberman)

6. Huberman as a young adult. (Courtesy of Rob Huberman)

7. *The Evening World* headline "Germany Declares War," announcing the start of World War I. (Wkimedia Commons)

8. Huberman in Palestine on Kibbutz Ein Harod, in a later photo. (Photo by Ida lbbeken, Courtesy of the Murray S. Katz Photo Archives of the Israel Philharmonic Orchestra)

9. Hitler at a rally in 1933. (Wikimedia Commons)

10. Jews forced to march with anti-Semitic signs in Germany in 1933. (Wikimedia Commons)

11. A Jewish shop with a Star of David, during Nazi boycott of Jewish shops in Germany in 1933. (Wikimedia Commons)

12. German conductor Wilhelm Furtwangler conducting in Berlin. (Wikimedia Commons)

13. Huberman's letter detailing fundraising and expenses for the Palestine orchestra. (From An Orchestra is Born - A Monument to Bronislaw Huberman)

14. Huberman and Albert Einstein, in a later photo. (Photo by John Huberman, courtesy of Joan Payne)

15. Hitler in 1935, the year the Nuremberg Laws were passed in Germany. (Wikimedia Commons)

16. Musician Lorand Fenyves, in 2000, an original member of the Israel Philharmonic Orchestra. (Photo by Peter Aronson)

17. Jewish residents being evacuated from the Old City in Jerusalem, in Palestine, during violence between Arabs and Jews in 1936. (Wikimedia Commons)

18. Chaim Weizmann and David Ben-Gurion, who helped Huberman establish his orchestra. (National Photo Collection of Israel, via Wikimedia Commons)

19. Jewish musicians and their families, on board a ship travelling from Europe to Palestine in 1936. (Courtesy of Murray S. Katz Photo Archives of the Israel Philharmonic Orchestra)

20. Jewish musicians, new members of the Palestine Orchestra, in 1936 after arriving in Palestine from Europe. (Courtesy of Murray S. Katz Photo Archives of the Israel Philharmonic Orchestra)

21. Huberman greeting conductor Arturo Toscanini in Palestine. (Wikimedia Commons)

22. Huberman congratulating Toscanini after a rehearsal in Palestine. (Courtesy of Murray S. Katz Photo Archives of the Israel Philharmonic Orchestra)

23. December 27, 1936, headline from *The Palestine Post* announcing Palestine Orchestra's first concert. (The Palestine Post)

24. A young Leonard Bernstein leading the Israel Philharmonic Orchestra in 1948. (Courtesy of Murray

S. Katz Photo Archives of the Israel Philharmonic Orchestra)

25. Zubin Mehta conducting the Israel Philharmonic Orchestra. (Photo by Oded Antman, Courtesy of the Murray S. Katz Photo Archives of the Israel Philharmonic Orchestra)

26. Street signs near the orchestra's theater named in honor of Huberman and Toscanini. (Wikimedia Commons)

27. Huberman and Toscanini in Haifa, Palestine, 1936. (Unknown photographer, courtesy of Murray S. Katz Photo Archives of the Israel Philharmonic Orchestra)

28. Poster advertising Palestine Orchestra concerts for 1937. (Courtesy of Rob Huberman)

29. Huberman boarding a plane. (Courtesy of Rob Huberman)

30. A Jewish family in Warsaw, Poland, in 1943, being marched by Nazis to deportation to a concentration camp. (Wikimedia Commons)

31. Zubin Mehta and the Israel Philharmonic Orchestra. (Photo by Shai Skiff, Courtesy of the Murray S. Katz Photo Archives of the Israel Philharmonic Orchestra)

32. Author Peter Aronson (Photo by Rashidah De Vore)

About Author Peter Aronson

Credit: Rashidah De Vore

I am a lawyer and writer living in New York City with my wife, Emily, and two teenage daughters. A few years ago, I realized my daughters and their friends were reading mostly fantasy, dystopian-type novels. With the real world so rich with the good, the bad and the unbelievable, I found this to be sad. I thought kids should be reading more reality-based books. So I decided to start writing books for kids focusing on real world people or issues – either through biographies or novels with a strong dose of reality.

I've never done anything this fulfilling. The Bronislaw Huberman book is the first of many books for kids that will be published in the coming months and years through my new publishing company, Double M Books Inc. The books all will be available through Amazon.com.

The Huberman book is the first in a series called The Groundbreakers: Short, inspiring biographies about transcendent individuals who take life to the next level, who overcome obstacles, fear and history to succeed against all odds. These biographies, illustrated with photographs, will focus on individuals, usually not household names, who rocked the world and shattered boundaries in arts, sports, politics, or other areas. These books are intentionally challenging for my target audience of middle-grade readers, ages 8 through 13.

My Mandalay Hawk series, for readers ages 8 through 14, will debut soon with *Mandalay Hawk's Dilemma: The United States of Anthropocene.* This is the first book in at least a trilogy of long-form novels about an unusually tenacious teenage girl and her friends who tackle monumental world problems – because no one else has succeeded in solving them. In the first book, peer into the near future as Mandalay Hawk goes after global warming. You'll discover what kid power really means. This is not a dystopian novel. This is reality based. Global warming is getting worse. The government is not doing anything to stop it. Someone has to step into the void.

I look forward to inspiring and educating kids and making them think, laugh and wonder for years to come.

Feel free to visit my website at
www.peteraronsonbooks.com or to email me at
peteraronsonbooks@gmail.com.

Thank you.

CPSIA information can be obtained
at www.ICGtesting.com
Printed in the USA
LVHW05s0345050718
582751LV00013B/267/P

9 781732 077515